BEST OF JUSTIN BIEBER

ISBN 978-1-5400-0402-4

7777 W. BLUEMOUND RD. P.O. BOX 13819 MILWAUKEE, WI 53213

In Australia Contact:
Hal Leonard Australia Pty. Ltd.
4 Lentara Court
Cheltenham, Victoria, 3192 Australia
Email: ausadmin@halleonard.com.au

Visit Hal Leonard Online at
www.halleonard.com

BABY

Words and Music by JUSTIN BIEBER,
CHRISTOPHER STEWART, CHRISTINE FLORES,
CHRISTOPHER BRIDGES and TERIUS NASH

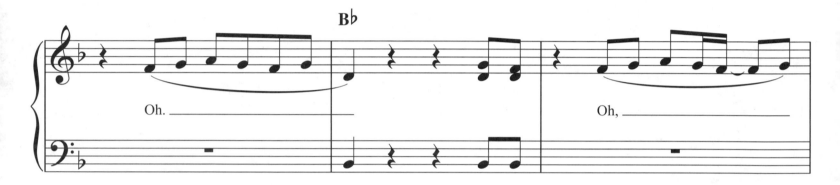

love, _____ you are my | heart, _____ and we will | nev - er ev - er, ev - er be a-

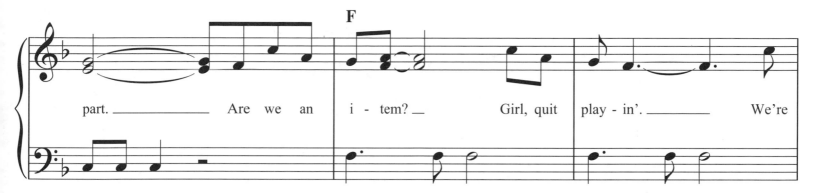

part. _____ Are we an | i - tem? __ Girl, quit | play - in'. _____ We're

just friends, _ what are you | say - in'? ___ Said there's an - | oth - er, and looked right in my

eyes. _____ My first | love broke my heart for the first ___ | time. And I was like,

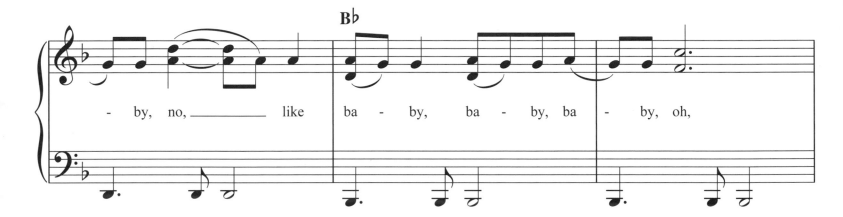

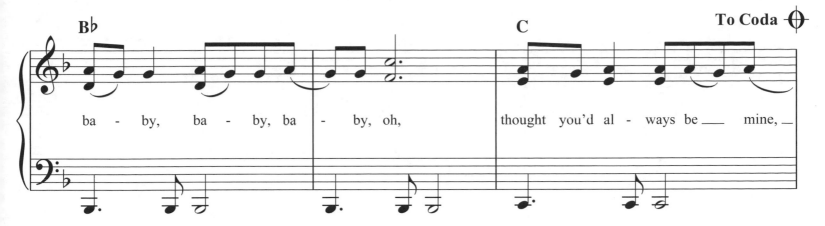

6

piec - es; _____ ba - by, fix me. And you shake me 'til you wake me from this

bad dream. _____ I'm go - ing down, ___ down, down, down, and I just

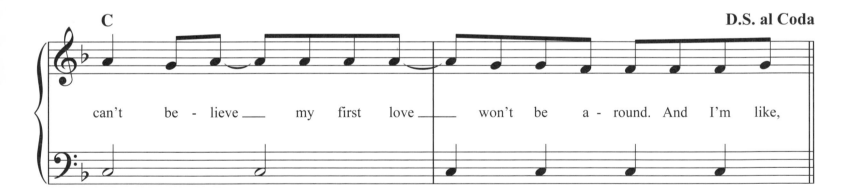

can't be - lieve ___ my first love ___ won't be a - round. And I'm like,

D.S. al Coda

_____ mine. ___

(Spoken:) When I was thirteen,
She made my heart pound, it skip a beat

I had my first love.
when I see her in the street and

ALL AROUND THE WORLD

Words and Music by JUSTIN BIEBER,
NASRI ATWEH, CHRISTOPHER BRIDGES,
ADAM MESSINGER and NOLAN LAMBROZZA

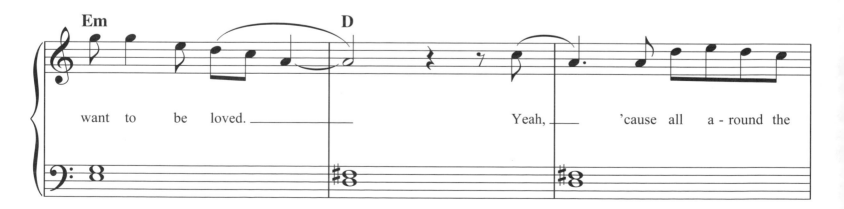

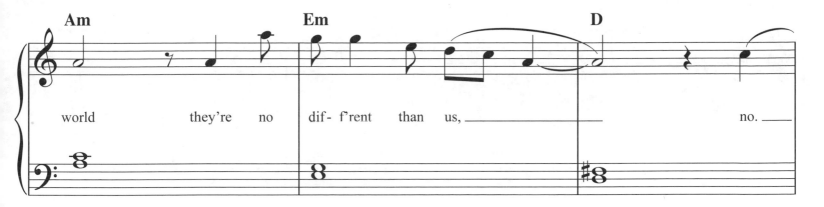

world they're no dif-f'rent than us, _____ no. ____

___ All a-round the world peo - ple want to be loved. _____

___ Oh, _____ all a-round the world they're _ no

To Coda

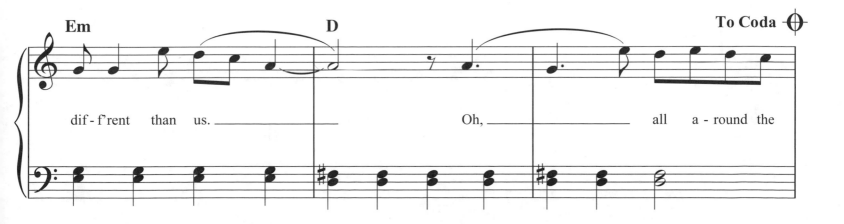

dif-f'rent than us. _____ Oh, _____ all a-round the

12

world. _____

All a - round the world.

1.

2.

You're

Am   Em   D

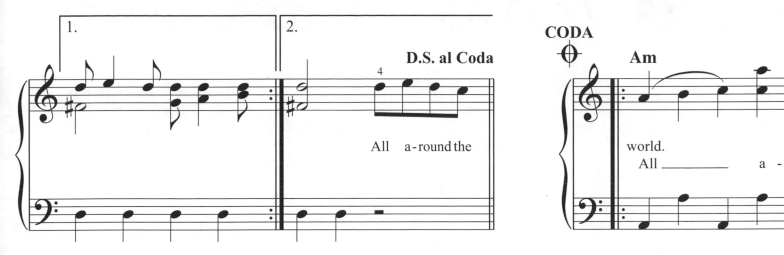

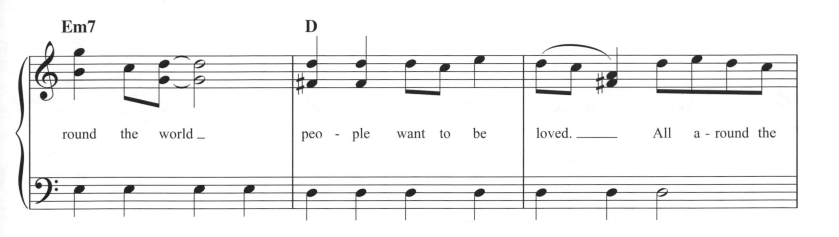

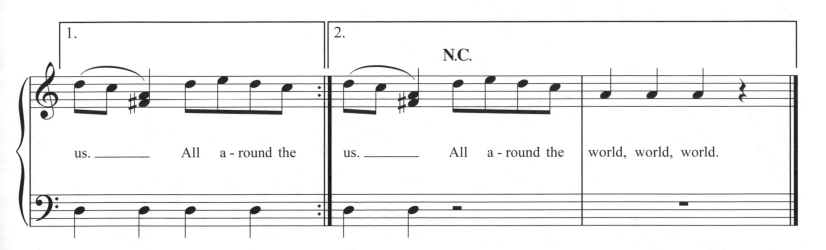

AS LONG AS YOU LOVE ME

Words and Music by JUSTIN BIEBER,
SEAN ANDERSON, NASRI ATWEH,
RODNEY JERKINS and ANDRE LINDAL

15

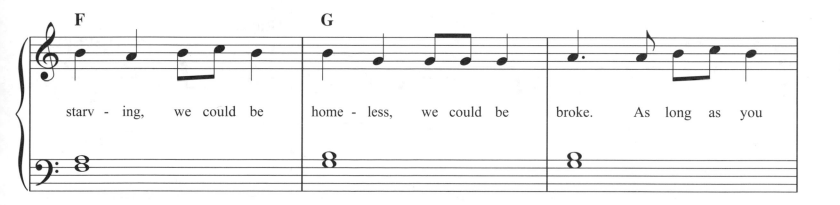

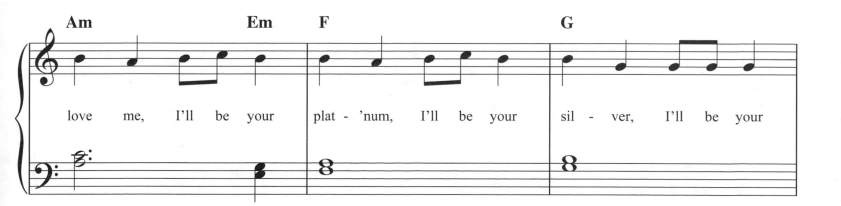

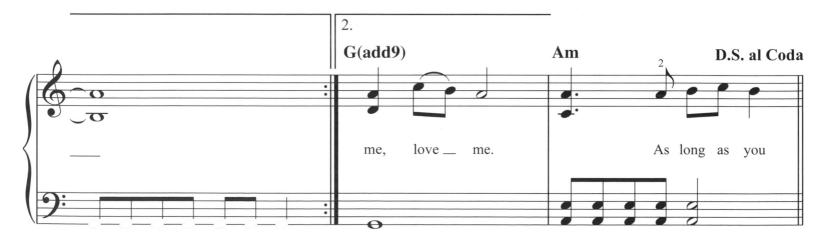

17

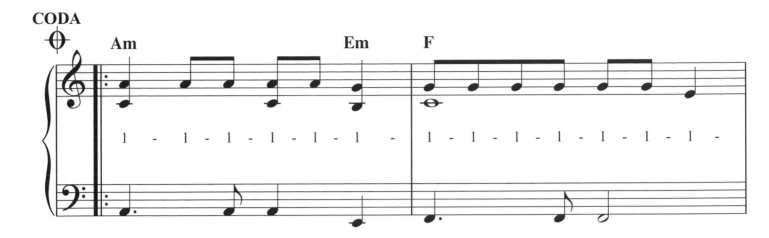

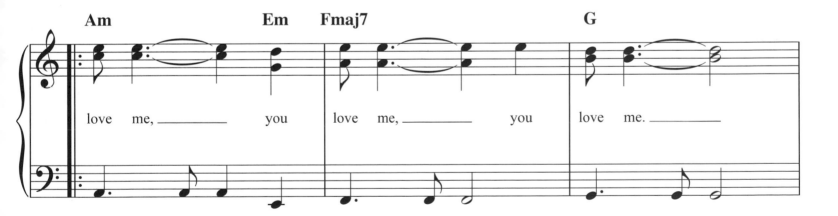

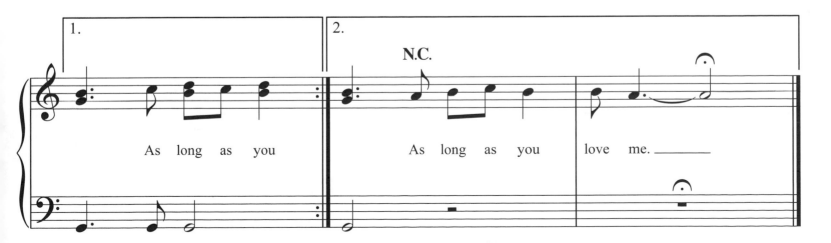

BOYFRIEND

Words and Music by JUSTIN BIEBER,
MAT MUSTO, MIKE POSNER
and MASON LEVY

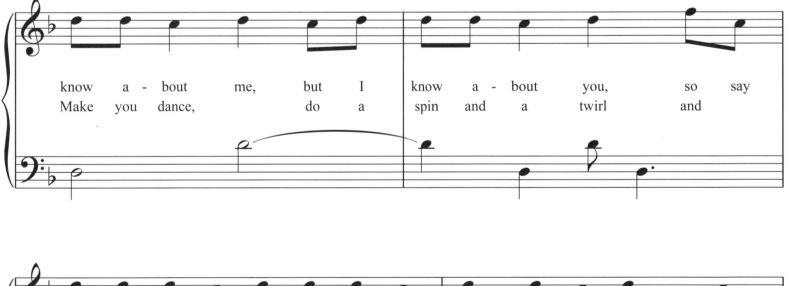

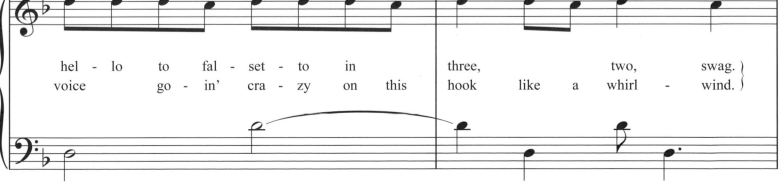

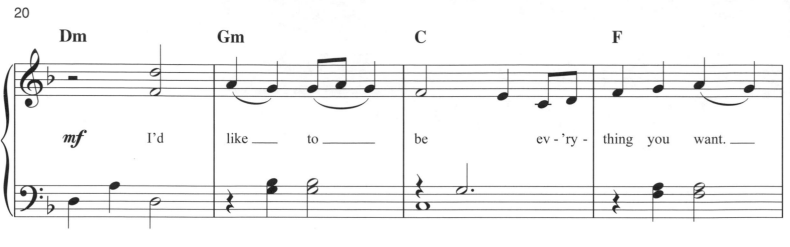

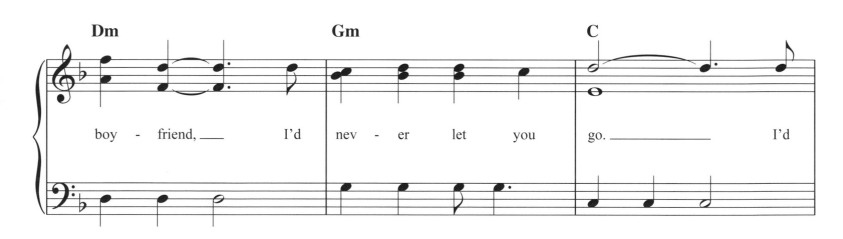

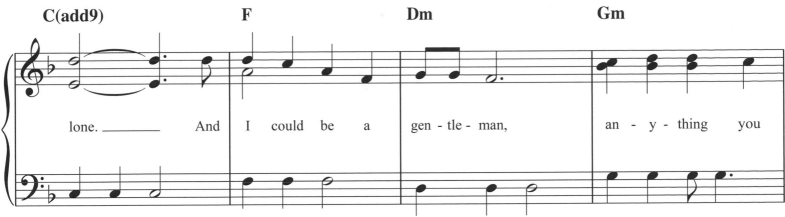

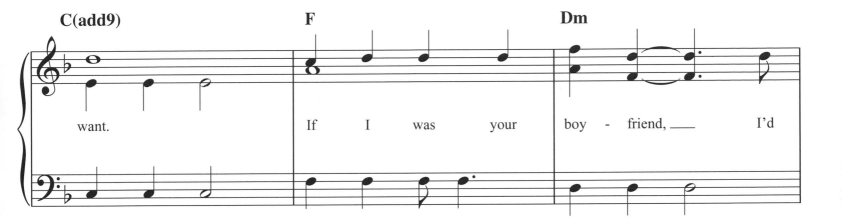

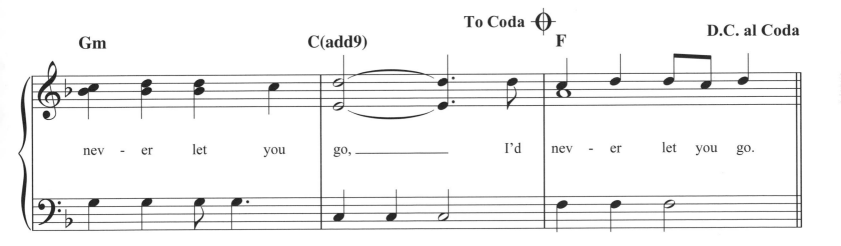

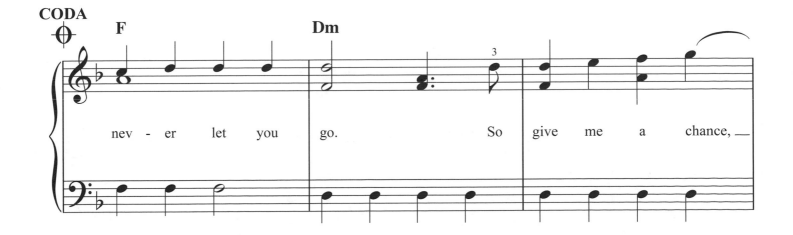

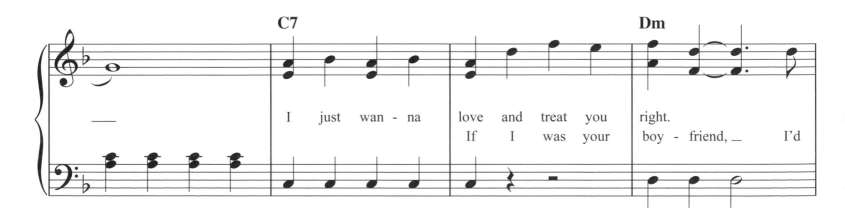

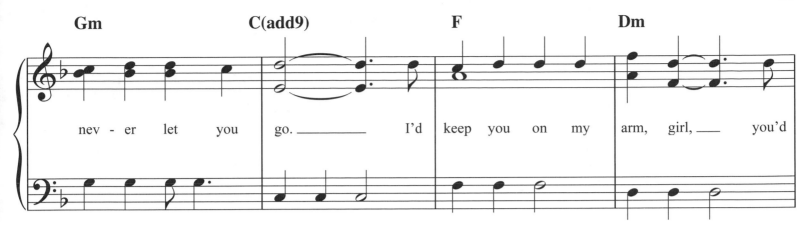

nev - er let you go. _____ I'd keep you on my arm, girl, ___ you'd

nev - er be a - lone. _____ And I could be a gen - tle - man,

an - y - thing you want. If I was your boy - friend, _ I'd

nev - er let you go. If I was your boy - friend.

SORRY

Words and Music by JUSTIN BIEBER,
SONNY MOORE, MICHAEL TUCKER,
JULIA MICHAELS and JUSTIN TRANTER

Moderately fast

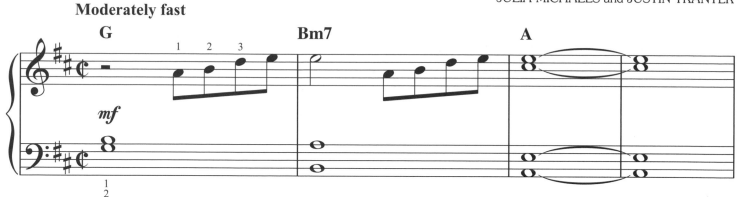

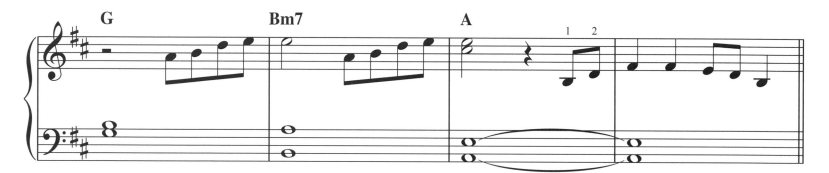

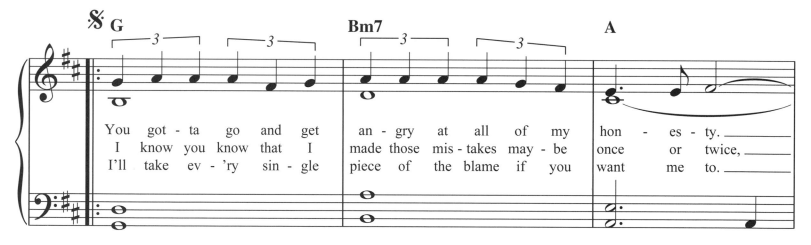

You got-ta go and get an - gry at all of my hon - es - ty. _____
I know you know that I made those mis - takes may - be once or twice, _____
I'll take ev - 'ry sin - gle piece of the blame if you want me to. _____

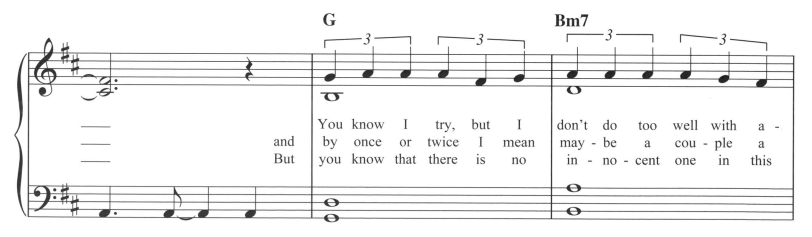

_____ and You know I try, but I don't do too well with a -
_____ by once or twice I mean may - be a cou - ple a
_____ But you know that there is no in - no - cent one in this

pol - o - gies. _____ I hope I don't run out of
hun - dred times. _____ So, let me, oh, let me re-
game for two. _____ But I'll go, I'll go, and then

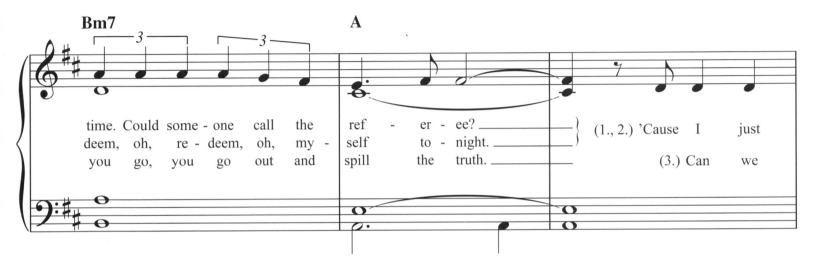

time. Could some - one call the ref - er - ee? _____ (1., 2.) 'Cause I just
deem, oh, re - deem, oh, my - self to - night. _____
you go, you go out and spill the truth. _____ (3.) Can we

1.

need one more shot at for - give - ness. _____
both say the

2., 3.

shot at sec - ond chan - ces. _____
words, say for - get this? _____ Yeah,

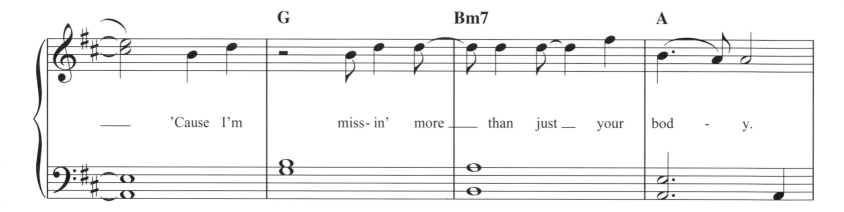

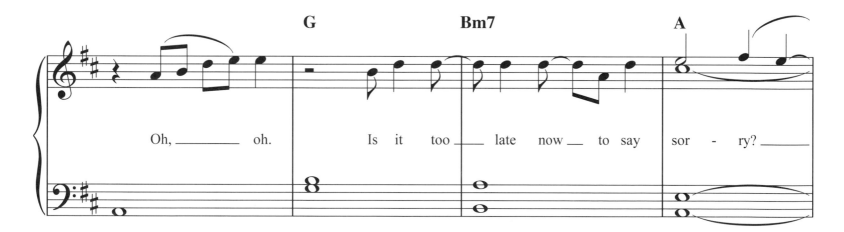

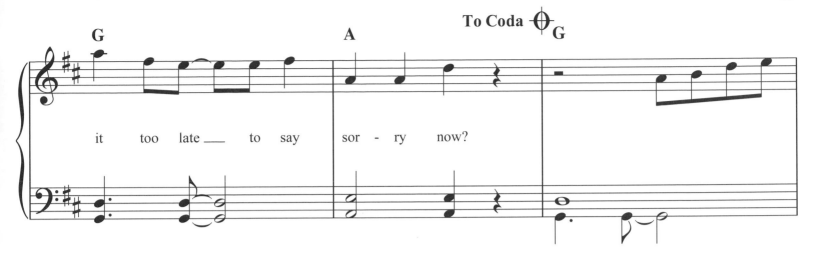

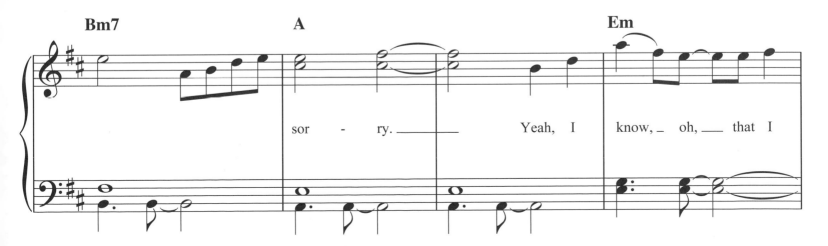

28

let you down. Is it too late ___ to say sor - ry now?

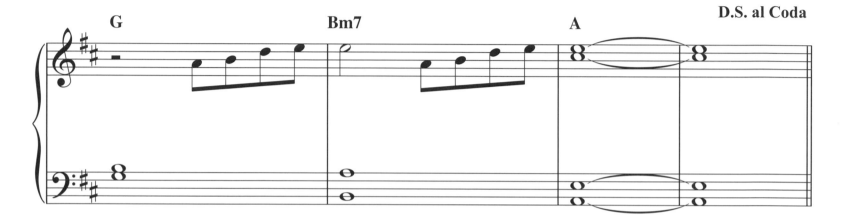

D.S. al Coda

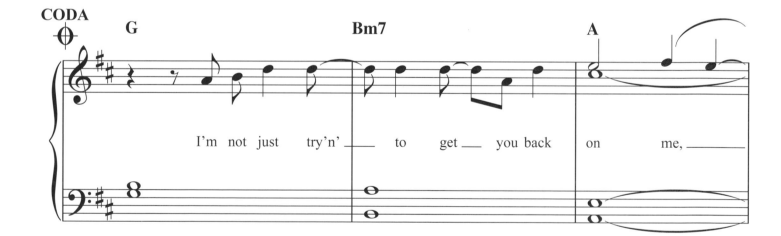

CODA

I'm not just try'n' ___ to get ___ you back on ___ me, ___

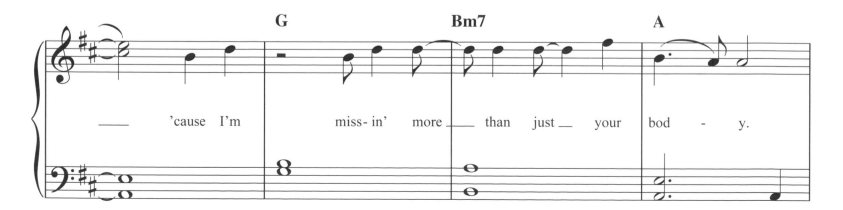

___ 'cause I'm miss- in' more ___ than just ___ your bod - y.

29

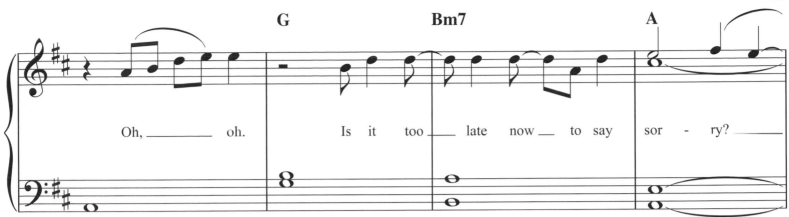

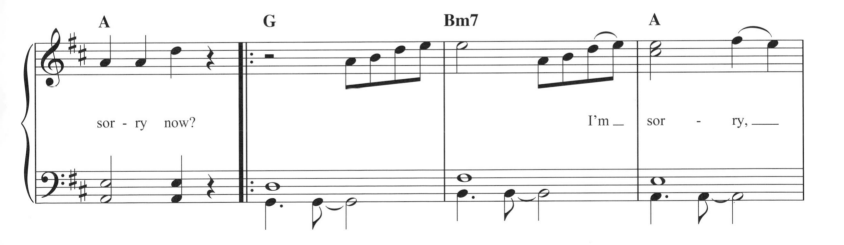

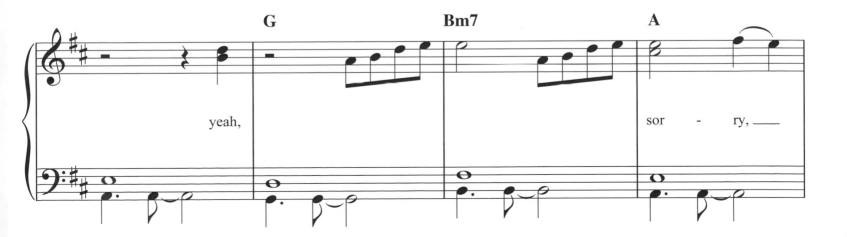

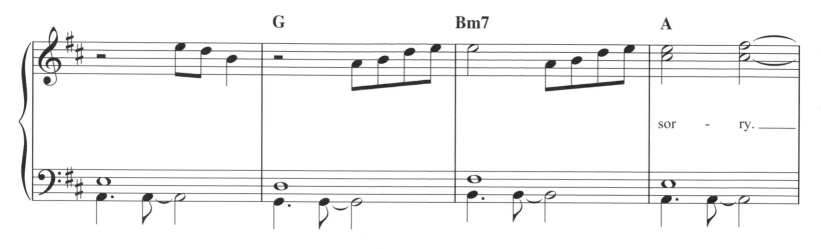

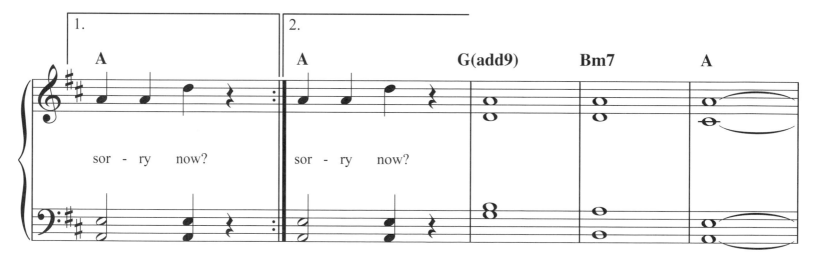

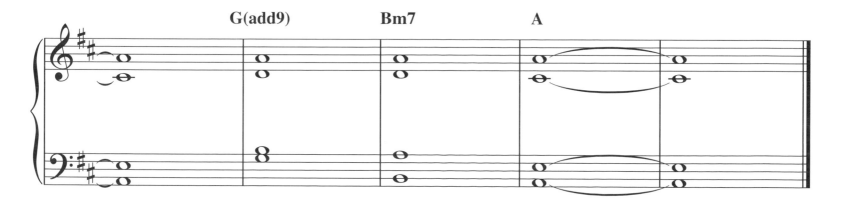

DESPACITO

Words and Music by LUIS FONSI,
ERIKA ENDER, JUSTIN BIEBER,
JASON BOYD, MARTY JAMES GARTON
and RAMON AYALA

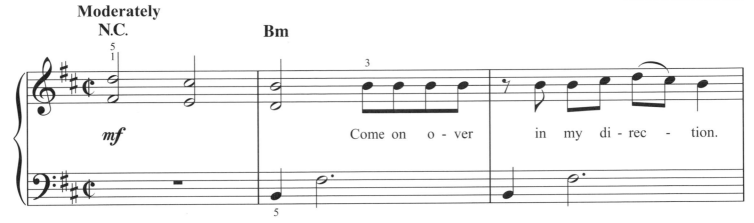

Come on o - ver in my di - rec - tion.

So thank-ful for that, it's such a bless - in', yeah. Turn ev -'ry sit - u -

a - tion in - to heav - en, ___ yeah. ___ Oh, ___ oh, you are ___ my sun-

rise on the dark - est day. _ Got me feel-in' some kind of way. ___ Make me wan-na

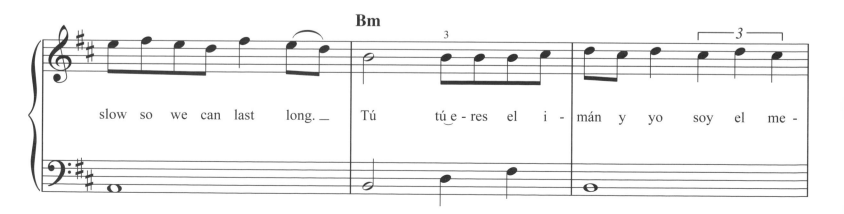

tal. Me voy a - cer - can - doy voy ar - man - do_el plan. Só - lo con pen

sar - lo se_a - ce - ler - a_el pul - so. Oh, yeah. Ya, ya me_es-tá gus-

tan - do más de lo nor - mal. To - dos mis sen - ti - dos van pi - dien - do más. _

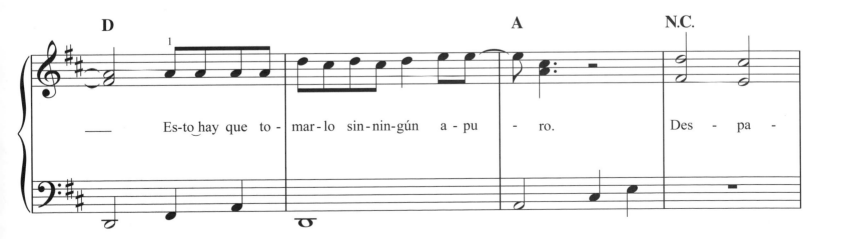

_ Es-to_hay que to - mar-lo sin - nin-gún a - pu - ro. Des - pa -

ci - to. Quie ro res-pi rar tu cue llo des - pa - ci - to. De - ja que te di - ga so-sas al o - í -

- do, pa - ra que te a cuer-des si no_es-tás con - mi - go. Des - pa -

ci - to. Quie-ro des-nu dar-te a be sos des-pa-ci - to, fir-mo_en las pa - re-des de tu la - be rin -

- to, y_ha - cer de tu cuer-po to-do_un ma-nu-scri - to. ____

Quie-ro ver bai-lar tu pe - lo, quie-ro ser tu rit - mo, que le en-se-nes a mi bo-

- ca, tus la - ga - res ___ fa - vo - ri - tos. ___

Dé - ja-me so-bre-pa - sar ___ tus zo-nas de pe - li - gro, has-ta pro-vo-car tus gri-

- tos, y que ol-vi-des tu a-pe - lli - do. Si te pi-do un be-so, ven

D

A

N.C.

lle - za en un rom-pe-ca - be - zas, pe - ro pa'mon - tar - lo a qui ___ ten-go la pie - za. O - ye!

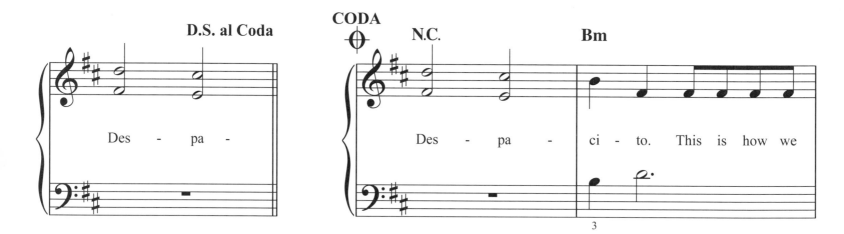

D.S. al Coda

Des - pa -

CODA

N.C.

Bm

Des - pa - ci - to. This is how we

G

D

do it down in Puer-to Ri - co. I just wan-na hear you scream-ing, "Ay Ben - di- to!" I can move for-

A

Bm

ev - er se que-de con - ti - go. ___ Pa - si - to a pa - si - to, sua-ve, sua-ve-

ci - to. Nos va-mos pe- gan-do po-qui-to a po- qui - to
Que le en se-nes a mi bo - ca,

tus lu-ga-res fa-vo-ri - tos. _____ Pa-si-to a pa- si - to, sua-ve, sua-ve

ci - to. Nos va-mos pe- gan-do po-qui-to a po- qui - to
Has-ta pro-vo-car tus gri - tos.

Y que ol-vi-des ___ tu a-pe- lli - do. Des - pa - ci - to.

LOVE YOURSELF

Words and Music by JUSTIN BIEBER,
BENJAMIN LEVIN, ED SHEERAN,
JOSHUA GUDWIN and SCOTT BRAUN

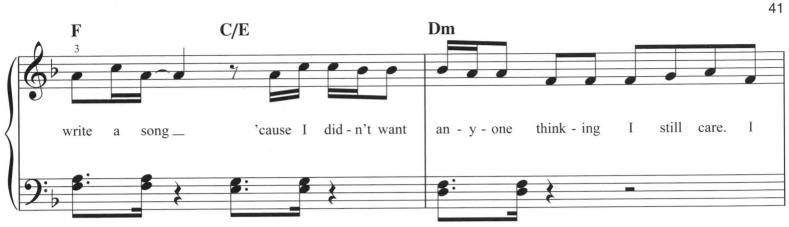

write a song __ 'cause I did-n't want an - y - one think - ing I still care. I

don't, but you still hit my phone up. And, ba - by, I'll be

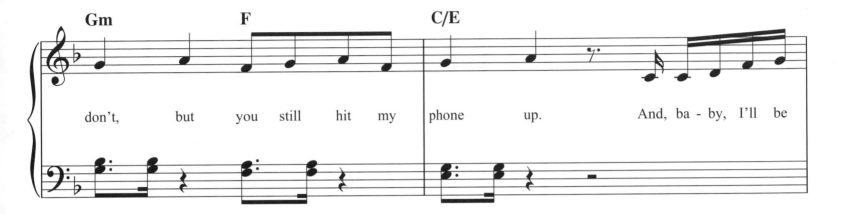

mov - ing on __ and I think it should be some - thing I don't want to

hold back, may - be you should know that. My ma - ma don't

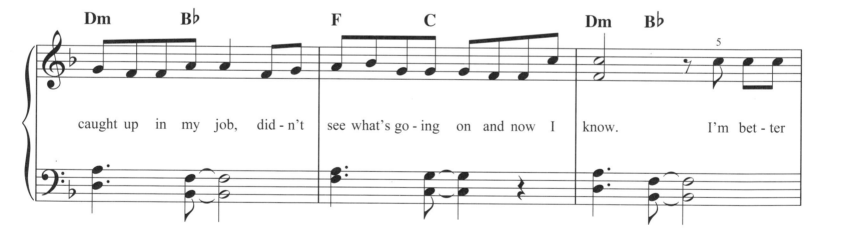

43

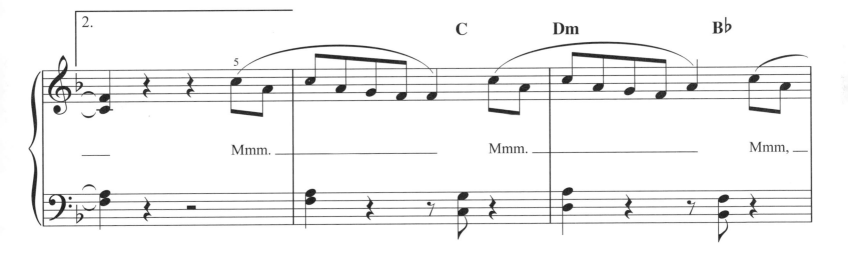

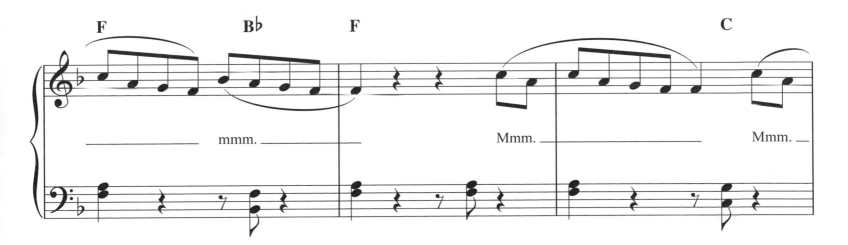

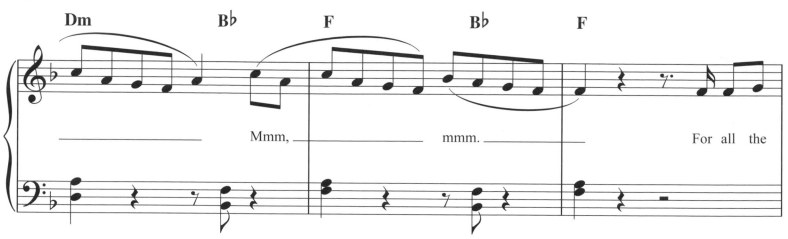

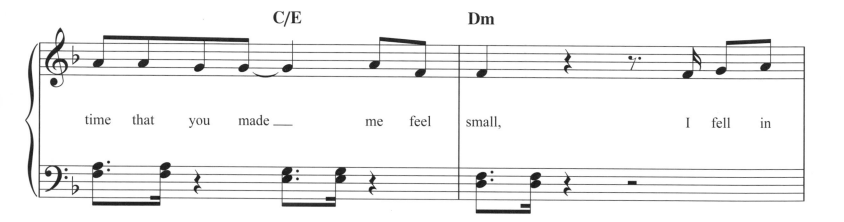

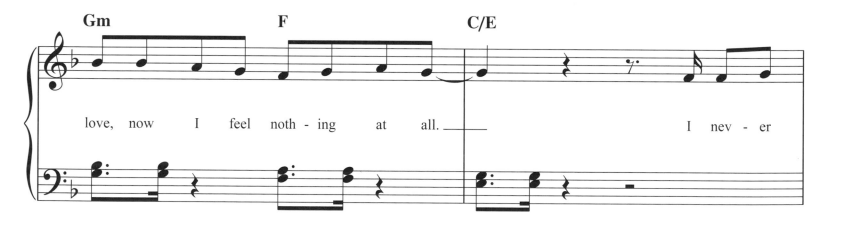

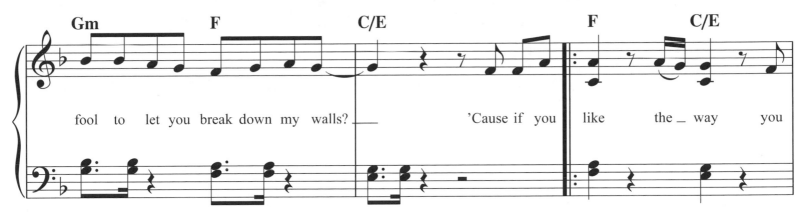

fool to let you break down my walls? ___ 'Cause if you like the __ way you

look that __ much, __ oh ba - by, you should go and love your - self. ___ And if you

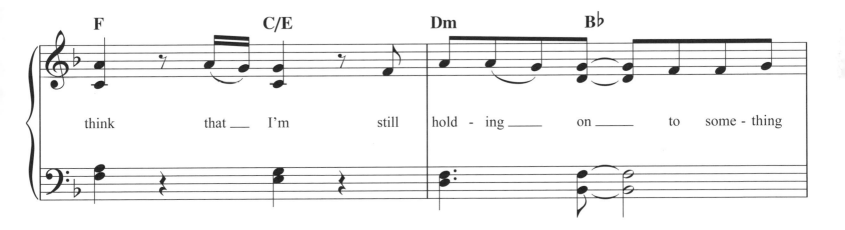

think that __ I'm still hold - ing ___ on ___ to some - thing

you should go and love your - self. ___ 'Cause if you

ONE LESS LONELY GIRL

Words and Music by EZEKIEL LEWIS,
BALEWA MUHAMMAD, SEAN HAMILTON
and HYUK SHIN

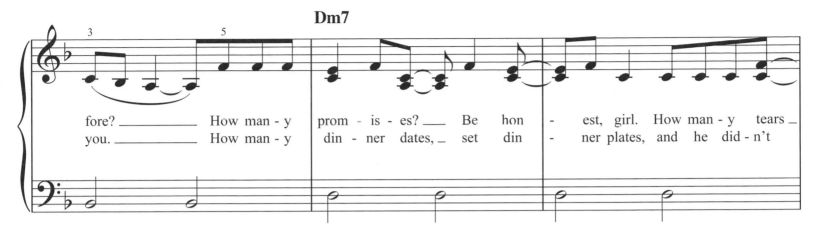

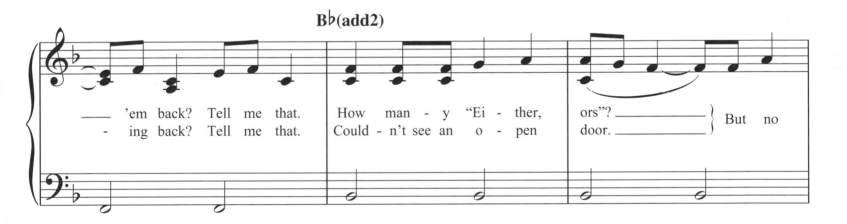

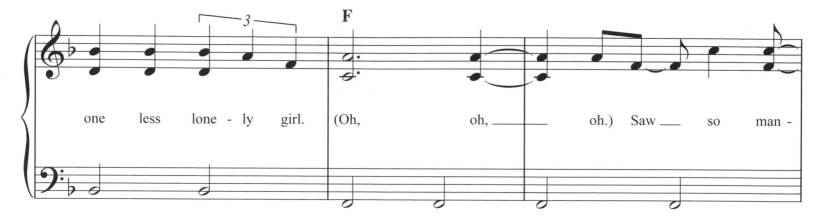

one less lone-ly girl. (Oh, oh, _____ oh.) Saw ___ so man-

B♭(add2) **Dm7**

- y pret - ty fac - es be-fore I saw you, _____ you. Now all___

B♭(add2)

___ I see ___ is you. ___ I'm com-ing for you. ___

F **B♭(add2)**

No, no, _____ don't need ___ these oth - er pret - ty fac-

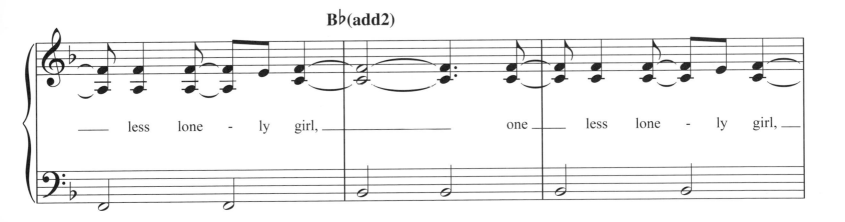

less lone - ly girl.   I'm gon - na put you first.

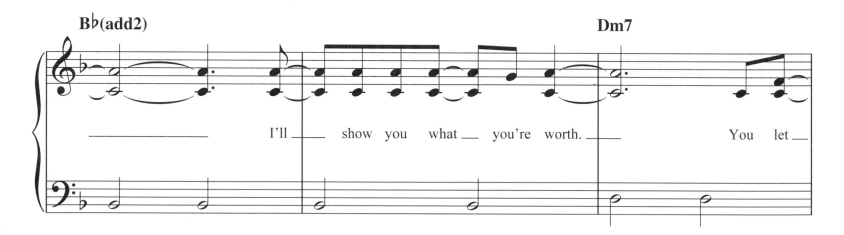

I'll show you what you're worth.   You let

me in - side of your world.   Christ - mas was - n't

There's gon - na be one less lone - ly girl.   I can

51

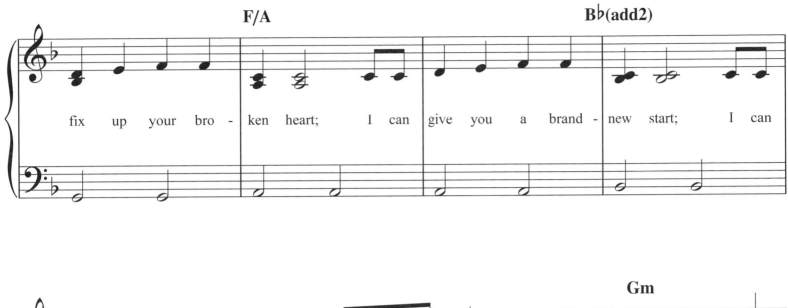

fix up your bro - ken heart; I can give you a brand - new start; I can

make you be - lieve. ____ I ____ just wan-na set one girl free to fall. Free

to fall (she's free to fall), fall in love __ with me. ____ Her heart's locked, and know

what? I've got the key. I'll take her, and leave the world with one ____ less... There's gon - na be one __

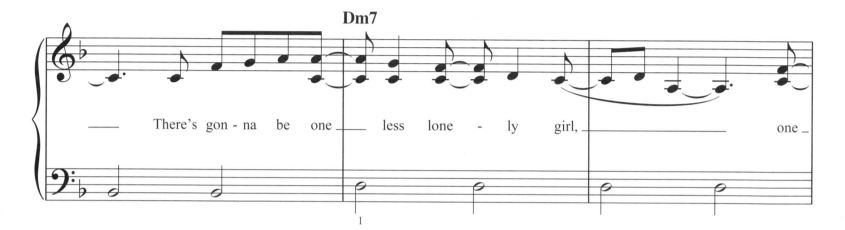

There's gon - na be one ___ less lone - ly girl. _____ I'm _

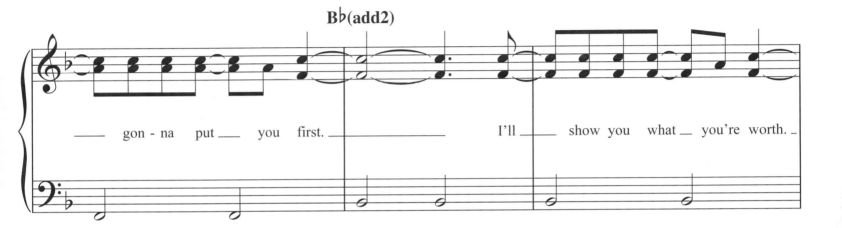

___ gon - na put __ you first. _____ I'll ___ show you what _ you're worth. _

_____ If you let ___ me in - side _ of your world, ___ there's gon - na be one _

_ less lone - ly girl. __ less lone - ly girl. __

ONE TIME

Words and Music by JAMES BUNTON,
CORRON TY KEE COLE, CHRISTOPHER STEWART
and THABISO NKHEREANYE

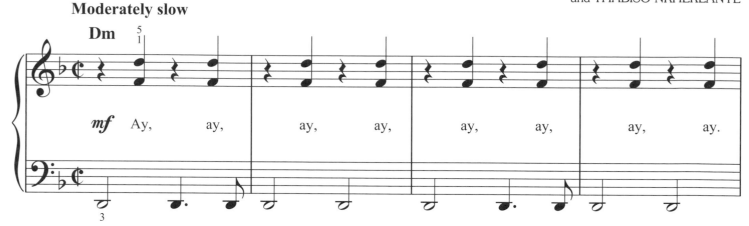

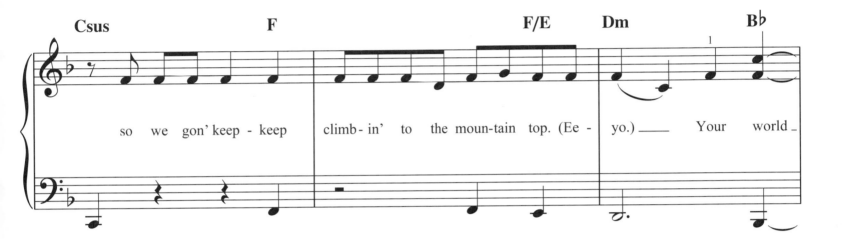

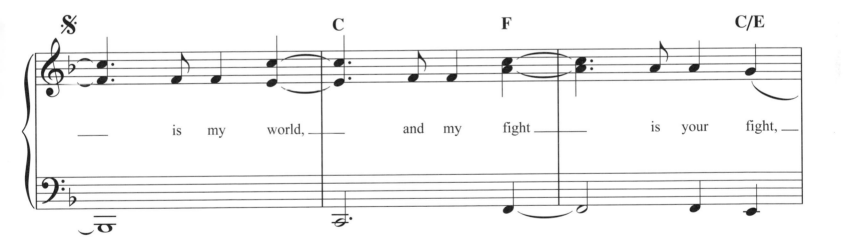

give it to _____ you. __ Your world __   love __ you.

Shaw - ty right there;   she's got ev - 'ry - thing I need. _____   And

I'm a - tell you one time, ___   (One time.) ____   give you ev - 'ry - thing you need, _

_____   down _ to my last dime. She makes _ me hap - py.

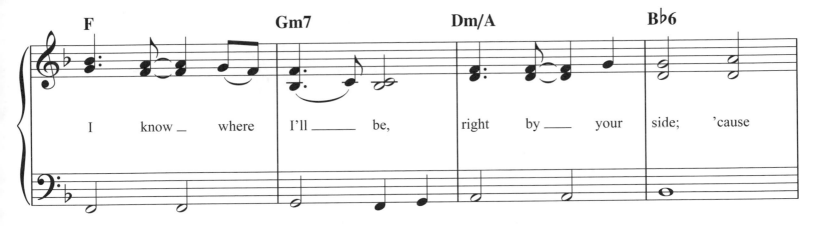

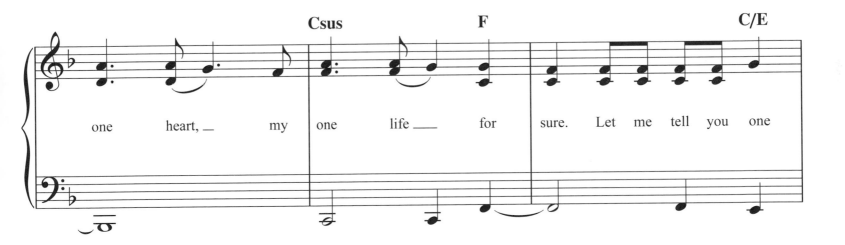

me plus you,

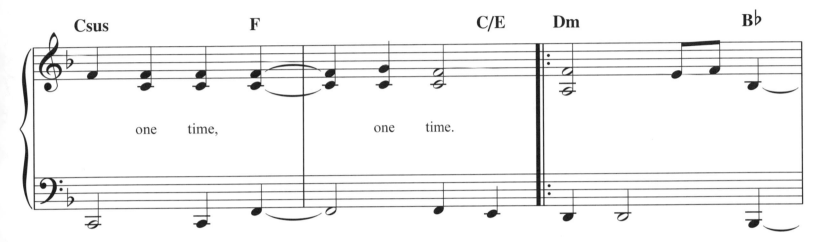

one time, one time.

SOMEBODY TO LOVE

Words and Music by JUSTIN BIEBER,
HEATHER BRIGHT, RAY ROMULUS,
JEREMY REEVES and JONATHAN YIP

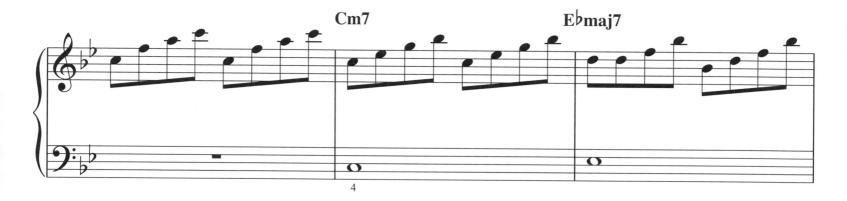

Cm

watch 'em play for ya. For you I'd be, _____ whoa, _____ ah, _____
smile for me, for smile for For me. I would take _____ ev - 'ry sec -

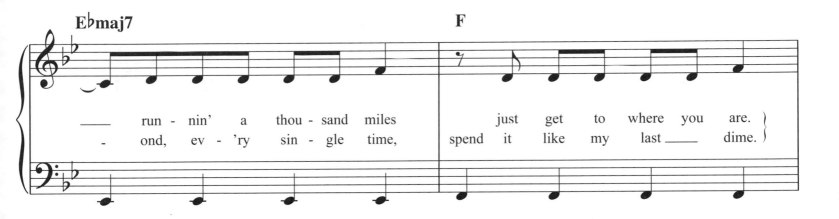

E♭maj7   **F**

_____ run - nin' a thou - sand miles just get to where you are.
- ond, ev - 'ry sin - gle time, spend it like my last _____ dime.

Cm7

Step to the beat of my heart. _____ I don't _____ need a

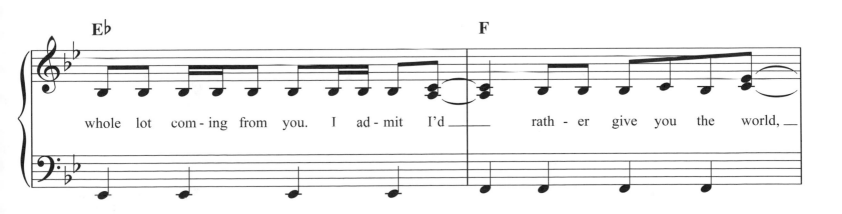

E♭   **F**

whole lot com - ing from you. I ad - mit I'd _____ rath - er give you the world, _____

or we can share mine. I know ____ I won't ____ be the

first one giv - ing you all this at - ten - tion. ____ Ba - by, lis - ten:

I just need some - bod - y to love. ____

____ I, I don't need too much, ____ just some -

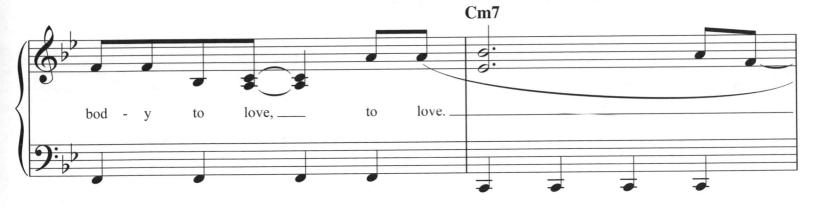

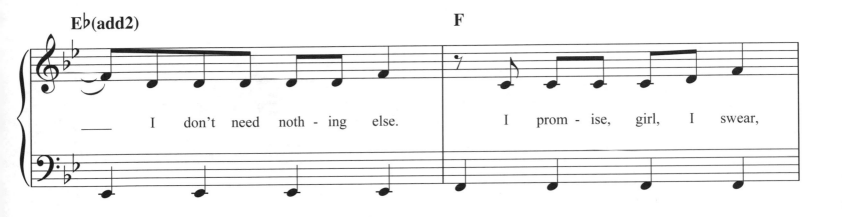

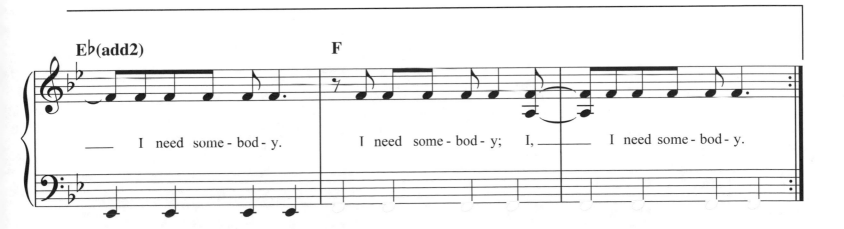

2.

Cm7

I just need some-bod-y to love. ____

E♭(add2)   **F**

____   I need some-bod-y;   I, ____

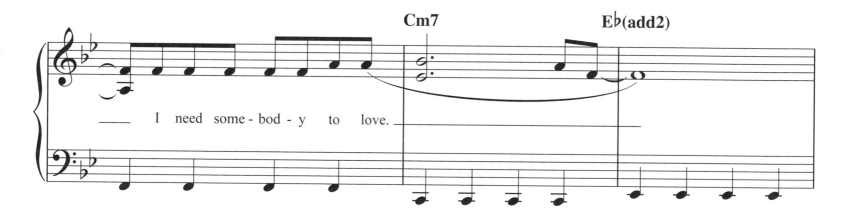

Cm7   **E♭(add2)**

____ I need some-bod-y to love. ____

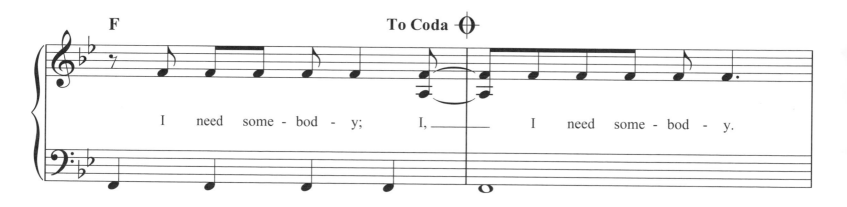

F   **To Coda** ⊕

I need some-bod-y;   I, ____   I need some-bod-y.

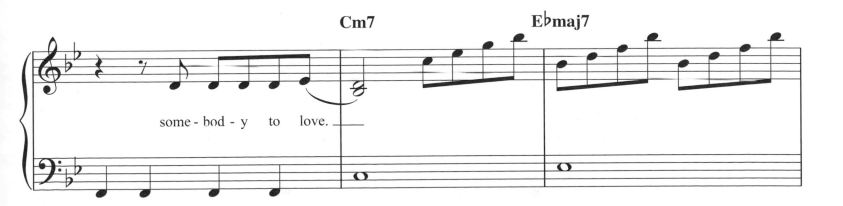

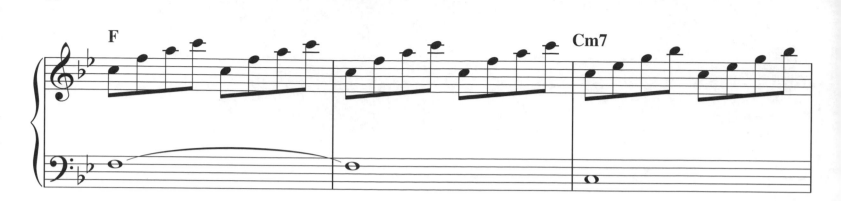

D.S. al Coda
(take 2nd ending)

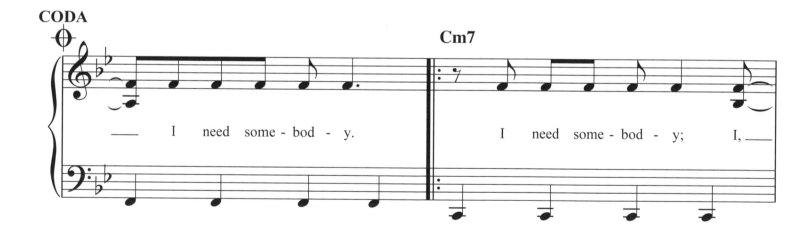

I need some-bod-y to love. ___

CODA

___ I need some-bod-y.   I need some-bod-y;   I, ___

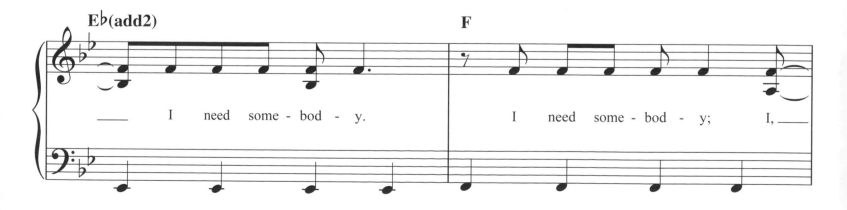

___ I need some-bod-y.   I need some-bod-y;   I, ___

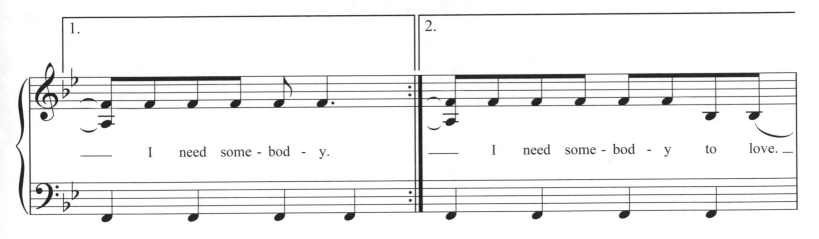

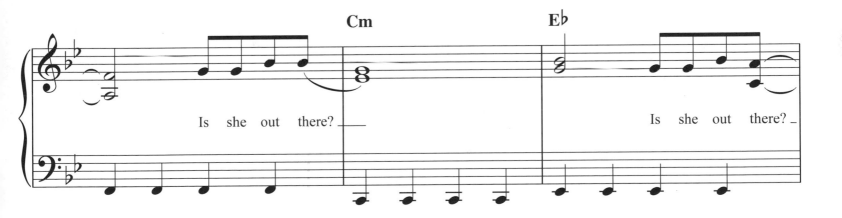

U SMILE

Words and Music by JUSTIN BIEBER,
ARDEN ALTINO, JERRY DUPLESSIS
and AUGUST RIGO

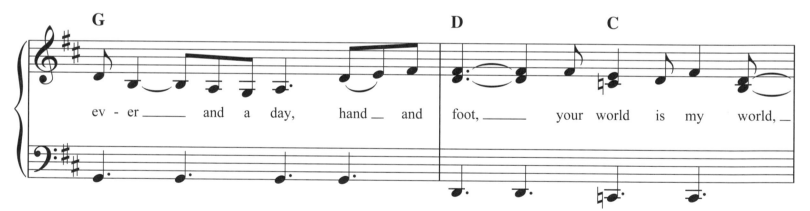

less than you should, ___ 'cause, ba - by: You smile, ___ I   smile. ___

_____ Oh, ___ 'cause when - ev - er   you smile, ___ I   smile. ___

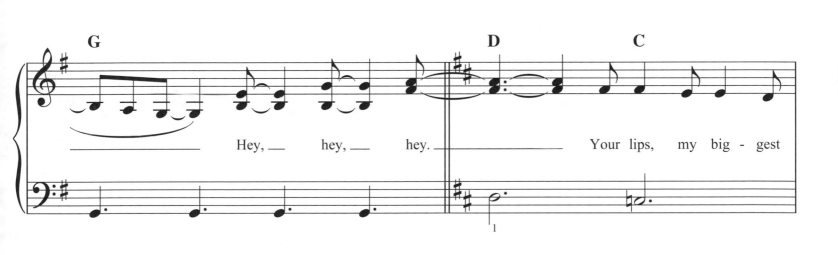

_____ Hey, ___ hey, ___ hey. _____ Your lips, my big - gest

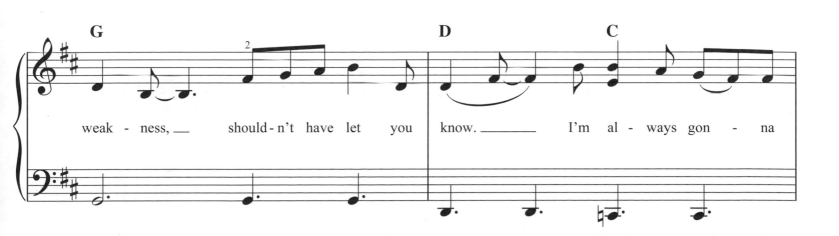

weak - ness, ___ should - n't have let you   know. _____ I'm al - ways gon - na

do what they say. _____ If you need me, ___ I'll come run - ning ___ from a

thou - sand miles a - way. _____ When you smile, ___ I smile. ___

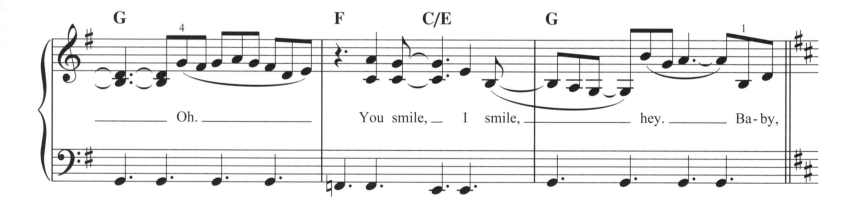

_____ Oh. _____ You smile, ___ I smile, _____ hey. _____ Ba - by,

take my o - pen heart ____ and all it of - fers, 'cause this is as

I smile, I smile, I smile. You smile, ___ I smile.

Make me smile. ___ Ba - by, you won't ev - er work for

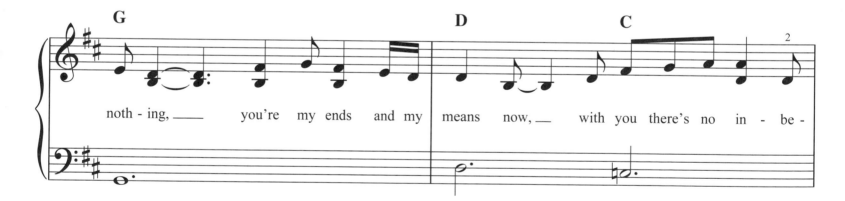

noth - ing, ___ you're my ends and my means now, ___ with you there's no in - be-

tween, ___ I'm all in. ___ 'Cause my cards are ___ on the ta - ble ___ and I'm

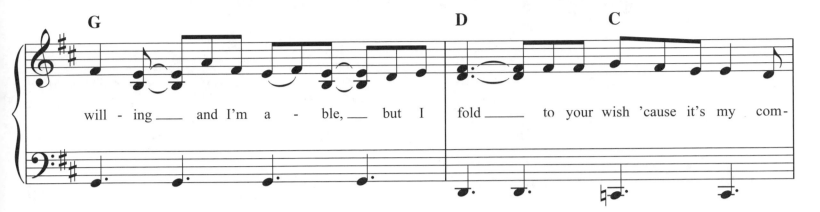

will - ing ____ and I'm a - ble, ___ but I   fold ____ to your wish 'cause it's my com-

mand, ____ hey, ___ hey, ___ hey.

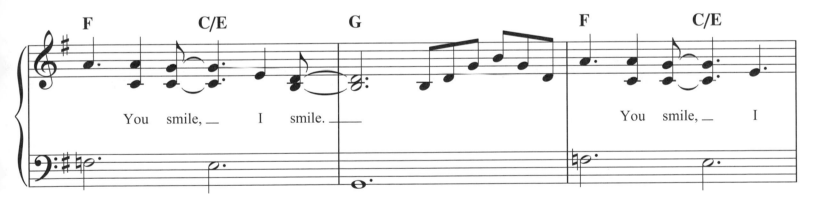

You smile, ___ I smile. ____   You smile, ___ I

smile. ____

8vb

WHAT DO YOU MEAN?

Words and Music by JUSTIN BIEBER,
JASON BOYD and MASON LEVY

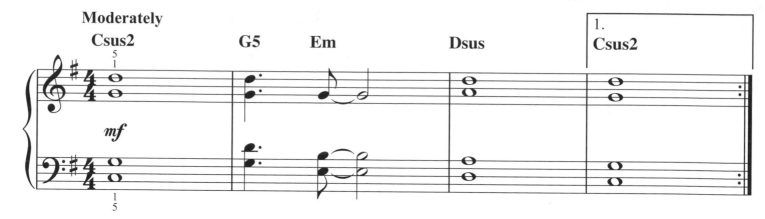

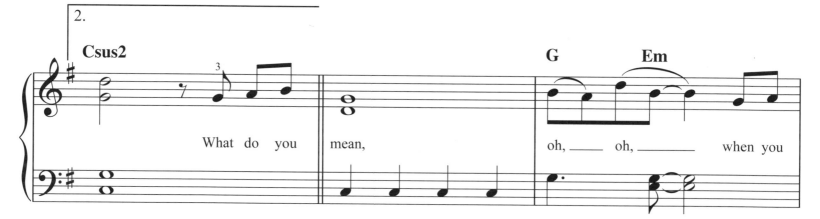

mean?   Oh, __ what do you mean?   Said you're

run - ning out __ of time, __ what do you mean?   Oh, __

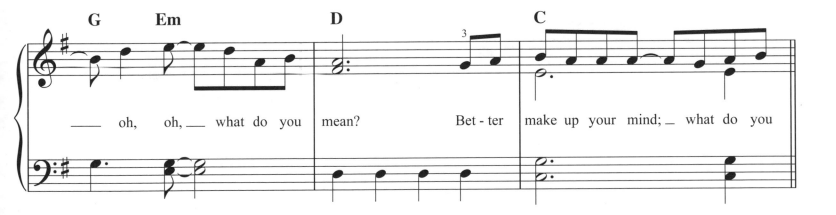

__ oh, oh, __ what do you mean?   Bet - ter make up your mind; __ what do you

mean?
mean?
You're so in - de - ci - sive what I'm say - ing. _____
You're o - ver - pro - tec - tive when I'm leav - ing. _____

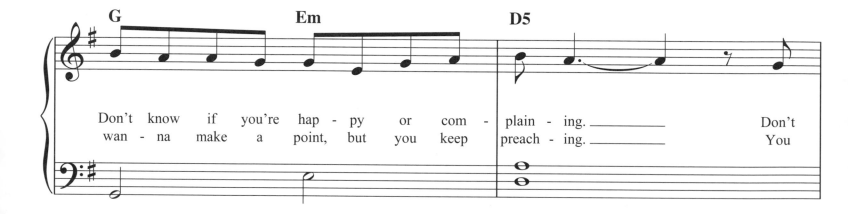

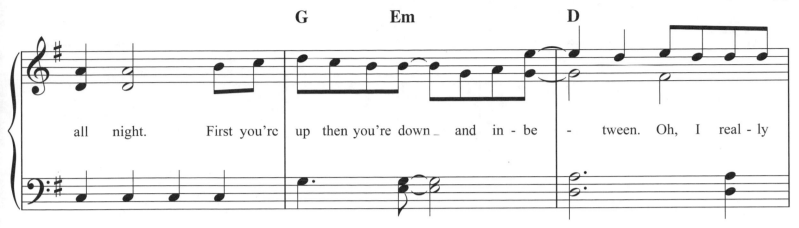

all night. First you're up then you're down and in be - tween. Oh, I real - ly

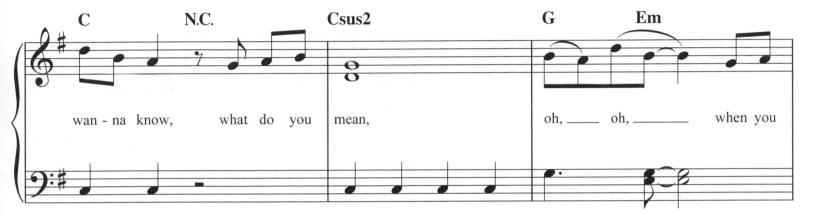

wan - na know, what do you mean, oh, ___ oh, ___ when you

nod your head yes, ___ but you wan - na say no? ___ What do you mean, hey, ___

___ yeah, ___ when you don't want me to move, ___ but you

tell me to go? __ What do you mean?

Oh, __ what do you

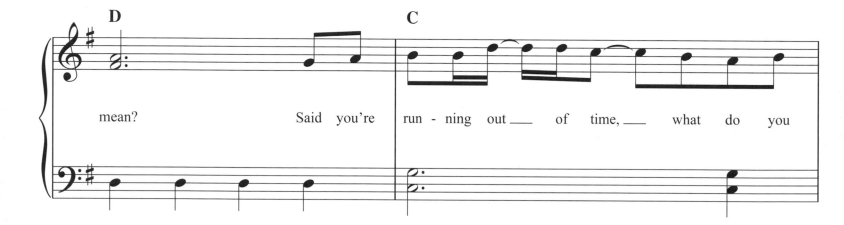

mean? Said you're run - ning out __ of time, __ what do you

mean? Oh, __ oh, oh, __ what do you mean? Bet - ter

1.
make up your mind; __ what do you

2.
make up your mind; __ what do you mean?